childhood experiences with the world is truly a privilege and will surely leave a positive impact on her readers. Living with a chronic illness can be challenging physically, emotionally, and spiritually. The pain and suffering that Charmaine endured over the years living with cell anemia is remarkable, but the love and support from family and friends allowed her to push through to achieve her goals. This book depicted inspiration of faith, hope, and restoration.

—Usha Foster-Becford, MSNPH, BScN, RN

Grace, the Girl with Cells that were Sickled is a must-read for anyone affected by SCD. The writing was captivating and interesting with very informative Dos and Do Nots for anyone afflicted by SCD.

—Miranda Theriault, RN, BN

This book, *Grace, the Girl with Cells that were Sickled*, hooks readers immediately with the disparities facing persons with sickle cell disease in a country that is lacking public medical resources. At last, a book with a set of practical, honest stories about a diagnosis and illness from someone of Caribbean descent. I love the dos and do nots of this book, especially the ones in chapters two and three. Chapter three brought tears to my eyes, as I was bullied in school by a few classmates and their older siblings who were from my home community. I could not imagine what Grace went through, being in physical pain and being bullied at the same time. The kindness and resilience of the siblings was astounding. The book provides gems for parents with children diagnosed with sickle cell disease, and they can also be applied to other childhood illnesses. This is a good read.

—Amoy Thompson, RN, BSN, MSN

I had the honour of reading *Grace, the Girl with Cells that were Sickled*. Charmaine was able to bring to life the challenges that some people with sickle cell face and the emotional toll those encounters can take on not just them, but their families and others within their surroundings. The story is true to its intended purpose. It educates the reader on what can be expected, what to do and not do, and how important it is to purposefully seek the information required when treating an illness and caring for those with an illness. It is filled with a wealth of information and is a great book for children and adults alike.

—Javel Burke-Douglas, RN, BSN, MClSc-WH

Resilient, hardworking, and dedicated are a few words that came to mind when I read this book about the life of Charmaine Brown. This book inspired me to believe in myself and remember the humble beginning as life evolved over the years. Charmaine sharing her

This book is dedicated to all my spiritual sons and daughters. I pray you hear my voice and spirit through these pages.

To my lovely wife Lisa for pushing me to get this book completed.

Last but definitely not least, my son Christopher, my youngest hero. I hope I make you proud and give you something to always remember me by. Love you so very much.

Introduction:

This book is not a book of 'cute' sayings but a book of 'jewels'. Each Empowerment Key is situational and contextual, that is to say that each 'key' does not apply to each and every situation. However, there is an Empowerment Key for each and every situation.

Use this book as a 'traveling companion'. Use this book as a daily source of inspiration and wisdom. Use this book as a tool to spark thought and contemplation.

The confessions are for you to rehearse. They are not that long so you can memorize them, become familiar with them, and most importantly use them. They are designed to spur you into a greater awareness and ACTION in being empowered in EVERY situation in your life! Enjoy!

1. Going to a new place is always more difficult than getting on an elevator to go to a higher level within the same building.

2. Your understanding is not a prerequisite for your obedience.

5-BE EMPOWERED!

3. You "do" from "who" you are...let Him change your heart (identity) so you can demonstrate a new heart, a new you, not just an outward behavior modification.

4. Don't be so fearful and apprehensive about that which has not come to past (and in a lot of cases will not) that you miss the opportunity to seize what you can BE.

5. In the midst of all the chaos and confusion, we MUST develop a keen sense of and a disciplined practice of: Hearing and Doing...there are always two components of creating an 'edifice' (which is you)...Hearing (planning/blueprints) and Doing (construction/building).

6. PROCESS, PROCESS, PROCESS.

7. Your level of receptivity is closely tied to your level of faith.

8. Resurrection is only powerful because death preceded it.

9. Seek to develop ministry "sons", not just members.

10. You don't have to know all the answers...but He does.

11. Self-pity is pride.

12.   Learn to put a 'period' at the end of a thing.

13.   Fear is walking in negative expectations, change your expectations you change what you get.

14. When we place a demand on God so that He gets the glory, we can move time in our favor.

15. As they were obedient, the water became wine. Do what He says do. Period.

16. God's environment is important to Him, and it should be important to us.

17. God has called us to not only hear His *word*, but His tone and cadence.

18.   Stop asking God to take you to new levels, and start asking Him to take you to new places and dimensions.

19.   PERIOD.

20.　Asking God to expand your influence and not expect to be tested is like trying to dry off with a wet towel.

21.   What you do and who you are, are not synonymous, but what you are will be seen by what you do.

22.   Fault-finders always find what they are looking for. What are you looking for?

23.   Aging and maturing are not synonymous.

24.   Being empowered is for those who want to get work done, not to have their ego stroked.

25.　The power of communication can overcome the problems of personality.

26.　Consistency and diligence can compete with talent and charisma.

27.　When you feel 'captured', trust God. Period.

28.　Leadership is not about glamor, it is sometimes grueling.

29.　Being empowered carries with it responsibility.

30. Empowered people sometimes take risks.

31. Live everyday knowing who you are.

32. When God equips you, He will also empower you.

33.   Don't be ashamed to be everything God has called you to be.

34.   Get into the presence of the Lord.

35.   Dwell in the presence of the Lord.

36. Obey the voice of the Lord.

37. Keep the commandments of the Lord.

38. Your level of growth and maturation is directly linked to your level of receptivity.

39.   DO NOT LIVE IN YOUR PAST failures OR victories.

40.   Love people.

41.   Forgive.

42.   Give.

43.   Invest.

44. Take your
     time.

45. Sometimes
     being the "2" is
     best.

46. Never give up.

47. Stay in the
     pocket.

48. Empower those around you, by doing so, you develop them and bless yourself.

49. Be yourself.

50. Don't waste your resources.

51. Love yourself.

52.   Serve God, not man.

53.   You will have what you expect and prepare for, even when you don't expect or prepare for anything.

54.   Be flexible.

55.   Learn to say, No.

56.   Keep yourself from 'strength drainers'.

57.   Invest in those who invest in you.

58. Don't forget you were not always where you are now.

59. Sacrifice.

60. Open the door for people literally and figuratively.

61. Never forget God.

62.   Learn to maintain excellence.

63.   Reformation takes time.

64.   Remember someone else may know more then you.

65. Don't forget, God doesn't fail.

66. Increase in integrity.

67. Love your enemies.

68. Show mercy.

69. Stay optimistic.

70. Sometimes you MUST encourage yourself.

71. Life isn't always going to be fair.

72. Before you start blaming the devil or someone else, consider your actions that caused the mistake to begin with.

73. Learn from your mistakes.

74. Teach others.

75. Instruct.

76. It's important to discern the motivation of those that you lead.

77. Don't waver in your commitment.

78.   Always allow people to make mistakes and grow.

79.   Keep loving.

80.   Never stoop to hatred.

81.   Maintain in the midst of adversity.

82. Learn when to regroup.

83. Use humility frequently.

84. Realize you don't have all the answers.

85. God forgives, so you can forgive yourself.

86. Learn to worship God.

87. Take a break.

88. Celebrate small victories.

89. There is a difference between gleaning and being a 'copy-cat'.

90.   Fear and faith are not opposites. Fear and faith motivate, lead and come by hearing; they simply lead in different directions.

91.   Don't let fear be your guiding light.

92.　Keep God first. Always. Period.

93.　Prioritize. Plan. Prepare.

94.　Maximize all opportunities.

95.　Keep a level head.

96.　Breathe.

97.　Persevere.

98.   Sometimes you must fight.

99.   Learn to cut your losses.

100. Chill out.

101. Somethings just aren't worth your time.

102. Realize everything has a cost, even if you didn't pay for it.

103. Help out when you can.

104. Show gratitude.

105. Use manners.

106. Don't stay mad
long.

107. Ask for help.

108. Learn to build
and fight at the
same time.

109. Stop being
offended.

110. Ask for help.

111. Learn to speak at the right time.

112. When life starts kicking your butt, turn around and kick back.

113. You are never by yourself.

114. RE-Calibrate.

115. RE-Calculate.

116. RE-Align.

117. Don't be afraid to say, "I don't know."

118. You have more in you that you realize.

119. Love hard,
pray often, give a
lot and "walk on
water."

120. Be a good
steward of your
resources.

121. Make it
happen.

122. Don't mistake taking a risk with a bad decision.

123. Meaningful and significant progress is gained through very hard work.

124. Someone understands you.

125. Know you
limits.

126. Take the time
to properly
prepare, plan and
execute.

127. Somethings will come into order when you decide on the direction you want to go in.

128. Losing friends can be painful, but sometimes necessary.

129. Sometimes you will never know the total impact you caused, KEEP doing good anyway.

130. PUSH yourself.

131. Don't be afraid to say, "Ouch!"

132. Wisdom shared is wisdom gained.

133. Don't just have character, demonstrate it.

134. Stretch yourself.

135. If someone is talking about someone else to you, they'll probably talk about you to someone else.

136. Make the most of every mistake, LEARN from it; don't just be embarrassed by it.

137. Somethings are better left unspoken.

138. MAINTAIN THE GAIN.

139. Don't stop praying.

140. The Lord isn't required to show you the 'hand' He's playing with, just trust that He may have an 'ace' up His sleeve and if not, "Oh well, you" have the best teammate.

141. Stop hiking the "Trail of Fears".

142. Be more considerate.

143. You have more in you then you think you do.

144. You'll never make the most out of life if you keep looking for and making excuses NOT to succeed.

145. Giving people
respect and honor
will cause favor to
come upon your
life.

146. Don't depend
on undependable
people.

147. Realize your parents aren't perfect, you aren't either.

148. Keeping your mouth closed can save you time and money.

149. Never think or
believe that
everyone is
against you.

150. Never think or
believe that
everyone is for
you.

151. Stay calm as best you can. Panicking creates an environment of instability and inefficiency.

152. Don't be afraid to judge a situation.

153. Fight to be settled.

154. Perceptions are peoples' realities. Change perceptions (minds) and new realities will be created.

155. Refuse to compromise your identity and godliness.

156. Know when it's time to stop crying.

157. Those who don't have control of their lives will always view themselves as victims.

158. That which brings you pleasure may cause discomfort to someone else, be careful and considerate.

159. Love is always appropriate.

160. Realize that we all don't communicate the same way.

161. In relationships, feed the other person(s) "you", not what they think defines you.

162. Lifting people takes more energy than tearing them down. Develop your muscles and start lifting.

163. Sometimes your kids are right and you are wrong.

164. <u>USE</u> your
resources wisely
and don't take
them for granted.
Learn the strength
of your resources.

165. You can yell in
the ear of a deaf
person and they
still can't hear
what you're
saying.

166. Trust must be activated.

167. The difference between dreamers and achievers is action.

168. Good days are not determined by events, but perspectives.

169. Choosey beggars often remain that way, beggars.

170. Wisdom is NOT inextricably linked to experience. One can be the most experienced, yet the one who needs the most wisdom.

171. The first
statement from a
fallen Nature was
a statement of
blame.

172. God is love.
But everyone you
love may not be of
God. Everyone
you love may not
be ordained by
God.

173. Learn to compliment people.

174. Realize when it's time to slow down.

175. People will always talk about you, whether you're doing good or bad. Stay consistent and steady.

176. God often uses the 'external' to stimulate that which is 'internal', be not afraid to allow what is outside of you to jump start your dormant strength and power.

177. Commitment is more than just a promise to stay or not to leave. It's a pledge to advance the mission of that which you are involved.

178. Don't give your temporary situation a permanent name.

179. Work it out.

180. Keeping your hand to the plow is vital for not only progress, but also for your healing and priorities.

181. If God has called you to be an eagle, don't identify yourself as a chicken. YOU were designed to soar above the clouds.

182. Never dismiss what you don't understand. Dig for understanding, you'll earn the respect of others.

183. Be honest, but don't count yourself out.

184. The Lord is with you, even at the times you don't feel Him. At times, He 'hides', but He is always there. KEEP it moving.

185. Use and maximize your resources; time, money and talents.

186. Being fired can be a blessing. Keep your head up.

187. Encouraging yourself has nothing to do with making yourself happy, but standing in and acting in courage.

188. Realize that it
is 'ok' to make
mid-course
adjustments.

189. Absence may
make the heart
grow fonder, but it
will also make you
more comfortable
with being a part.
Be careful.

190. Your comfort can kill you.

191. Laugh loudly and excitedly.

192. Never make decisions based on your own 'press'. Some hate you. Some love you. Make the best decision.

193.   Relationships are like navigating through a river. Sometimes it's easy to progress, sometimes it's hard to progress. Sometimes the waters will get in the boat. Sometimes it will be 'shifty', but whatever the condition is at the moment, being equipped and empowered with love and forgiveness you can always keep your head above water.

194. Wives are valuable.

195. Husbands are vital.

196. Children are blessings.

197. Siblings are life-savers.

198. Parents are priceless.

199. Re-invent your relationship.

200. In families not everyone will see the same thing the same way, but if the MISSION is clear, progress can be made.

201. Being a change agent in your family may be lonely, but it may be necessary.

202. Wishing things would be different is not the same as making things different. If you have the desire to see change, you can cause great change to occur.

203. No one gets out of life alive. Ensure that you are preparing and empowering the generations after you.

204. To honor your parents does not mean you have 'warm fuzzy' feelings toward them, but that you DEMONSTRATE respect, not feel it.

205. Prayer is not only good for your family, your church, but also your business.

206. Plan on ways to show and express love, not just receiving it.

207. Children aren't perfect. Parents aren't perfect. Christ is perfect.

208. Out of the same loins can come two "nations". Know it. Embrace it. Discern it.

209. Being dysfunctional does not necessarily disqualify you, it just increases the urgency for you to become functional, people are waiting and depending on you.

210. Learn to grow and develop with those you are in relationship with. No one stays the same. Give each other space to grow and develop without condemnation and spite.

211. Learn and discern when an individual stops valuing your presence in your life.

212. Marriage is not a sprint to the finish line. Marriage is a marathon built on endurance and satisfied thirst.

213. Seasons of pain visit everyone at different times. Be sensitive to people, your season is coming.

214. The more you love, the more you grow.

215. Maintain relationships with those who "feed" you themselves.

216. People just don't operate in gifts, people ARE gifts.

217. When those given to your charge prosper, you prosper.

218. Acknowledge and appreciate your relationships.

219. Relationships are grown and are the healthiest when there is good and bad experiences.

220. Keeping your word within your relationships not only builds credibility, it also causes discipline to grow and develop, thus making you more valuable.

221. Offenses will come, but so will forgiveness, if you let it.

222. Bitterness in any form is NOT the will of God for your life.

223. Refuse to repeat the mistakes and curses of your previous generations, without becoming bitter toward those that perpetuated the "crimes".

224. The release and expression of the anointing is developed through tests and trials.

225. YOU have the power in YOU!

226. Never stop moving ahead, even if slowly.

227. Rolling with the punches is good, but, sometimes it's time to stop rolling with them.

228. Whatever you continue to justify, you give allowance to have free course in your life.

229. Life is short. Life is special. Life is sacred.

230. Pay attention to your dreams. Dreams are 'revealers' of what's inside you.

231. Look for and develop 'win-win' situations.

232. Spend less time talking about those who have offended you, and more time talking to them.

233. The sexiest thing you can do for your spouse is meet their needs.

234. There is a difference between a whiner and a winner. Which are you?

235. If you bail out when you have work to do, you cannot expect to enjoy the benefits of that work.

236. Surround yourself with people who challenge you to advance.

237. One of the most authentic signs of a true leader is courage.

238. Listen to the
     Holy Spirit.
Period.

239. Mistakes will
     be made, but the
     mistakes don't
     have to 'make'
     you.

240. You will only
    operate at the level
    you see yourself
    in.

241. For power to
    be effective, it
    must be
    harnessed.

242. Intimidation
      and insecurity
      walk hand in
      hand, you get rid
      of the one, and
      you'll most likely
      get rid of both.

243. Love
      empowers faith.

244. Leading others will cost you your life.

245. No one can replace you; they can just do what you do. You are irreplaceable.

246. Discern 'kairos' (spontaneous, qualitative) moments.

247. The Lord calls and appoints.

248. Confidence and arrogance are not the same.

249. Read. Ask
    questions. Learn.
    Grow.

250. Fill your
    relationship
    'coffers' with the
    treasures of
    invaluable
    resources.

251. Dig deep with the rich soil of your buried experiences. You will find 'rocks' that can keep you stable in your present and future.

252. The devil may
   be in the details,
   but so are the
   strategies to
   overcome him.

253. People will
   value or devalue
   you in direct
   proportion to what
   you
   subconsciously
   show them.

254. If you did your best, you have nothing to be ashamed of. Grow from it.

255. There is no such thing as the 'impossible'.

256.   When we argue it's generally because we have birthed "flesh babies", that which is of the flesh is flesh, that which is of the spirit is spirit. We must give birth again, but to "spiritual babies". "Spiritual babies" resolve problems birthed out of our flesh.

257. Drive a different way to work. Go home a different way. Do something new.

258. Take a vacation.

259. Rearrange the furniture in your house.

260. Fast on behalf of someone else.

261. Treat people with consideration.

262. "The Relationship Tripod": Respect. Selflessness. Communication.

263. Chase the
      presence of God.

264. Peace is a
      condition, not a
      feeling.

265. Always and in
      all ways upgrade
      in godliness.

266. Never, never, never make the mistake of thinking you know it all, you don't. Period.

267. Mercy begets mercy.

268. Faith is the engine of force (substance) and instrument (evidence) that creates the environment for the unseen to manifest.

269. A knuckle-head is an individual that is short on thinking and exhibits the inability to expand their thoughts. Don't listen to knuckle-heads. Period.

270. Don't let a bad day define the rest of your week.

271. Just because you're anointed, does not mean you are in order.

272. Don't hold people hostage to their past, you could be missing on your freedom and deliverance.

273. You may be surprised at the response you would receive from people when you treat them as the person they are and not the way you feel about them.

274. Revelation sometimes comes uninvited.

275. You can never go wrong walking in love.

276. Integrity is valuable, even in families.

277. Magnify the solution, not the problem.

278. Don't view responsibility as an obligation, view it as an opportunity to respond and display your abilities.

279. Hurt people may hurt people, but healed people take on the responsibility to heal people.

280. Be a starter.

281. Initiate your progress. Take the onus of your own success.

282. Light the way for someone else.

283. Don't only tell the truth, live the truth, be the truth.

284. Make lemons into lemonade, turn sour grapes into grape juice and don't walk on banana peels.

285. When faced with adversity, allow your untapped strength to display itself.

286. Planning ahead is great, but don't get too bogged down with the planning that you become paralyzed into inaction.

287. Safety is in the multitude of counselors, but some counselors are fools, be careful.

288. Remarkable feats are accomplished by remarkable efforts.

289. Events sometimes mark significant times in history, but let repentance and a change of mind mark the beginning of a new life.

290. The Lord
knows what we
don't know, but
will reveal
wisdom,
knowledge and
His will in prayer.
Pray.

291. You can't have
a positive impact
without positively
touching and
being intimate
with someone or
something.

292. In order to advance, there must be an impact on your present and future. Your present thoughts must see your future and begin to program your attitude to walk it out.

293. Be very careful who you link up with.

294. Get rid of pride and increase your love.

295. Reconcile as best you can.

296. Stop thinking that what you're going through is about you. You have 'nations' and 'generations' in your 'womb'.

297. Get over it. Quickly.

298. God can protect you from those you thought were in your corner. Be encouraged.

299. Clean your car and your house. They are reflections of you.

300. Shake yourself from mediocrity.

10 Power Confessions

1. Personal
2. Self-Esteem
3. Finance
4. Health
5. Relationship
6. Parenting
7. Professional
8. Forgiveness
9. Addiction
10. Future

1-I boldly confess that I am full of power. I have everything I need that pertains to life and Godliness. I confess that I am Godly and content. I declare I have received great gain. I confess and declare that I can do all things with and through Christ which strengthens me. I boldly confess and declare that I am a victor and never a victim. I confess that with God all things are possible. I declare that I have received power, love and a sound mind. I have peace. I have love. I walk in power.

2-I boldly confess that my self-esteem is healthy. I boldly declare that I am fearfully and wonderfully made. I boldly declare that I did NOT receive the spirit of bondage again to fear. I boldly declare that I have NOT been given the spirit of fear. I boldly declare that I have been accepted in the beloved. I boldly declare that I am seated with Christ in Heavenly places. I confess that I see myself as God sees me. I boldly declare that by the GRACE of God I am who I am, and God does NOT make a mistake. I boldly declare my life is a blessing to others. I boldly declare that I will walk in confidence. I boldly declare that my self-esteem is whole. I boldly declare that God loves ME.

3-I boldly confess and declare that all my needs are met according to God's riches and glory. I confess and align myself with the law of sowing and reaping. I boldly declare that I am a giver. Since I am a giver, men give into my bosom. Since I am a tither, doors of opportunity are opened for me because the seed eater and devourer are consumed on my behalf. I declare that God has given me the power to get wealth. I am not lazy, slothful in business or dishonest in my business, therefore I will prosper for generations to come. I declare that I am a good steward over the Lord's resources and the Lord takes pleasure in prospering me.

4-I boldly declare that it is not God's will that I be unhealthy. My body is the temple of the Holy Ghost. I declare that discipline is my portion. I declare that I do not eat out of boredom or compulsion. I declare I eat to live and do not live to eat. I discipline my body that I can live a long life of health and prosperity. I do not feed my body with harmful toxins. I declare that my body belongs to God. I declare that my days are filled with peace bodily, emotionally and spiritually. I declare that I am whole and healthy in every area of my life.

5-I boldly confess and declare that my relationships are healthy and not toxic. I declare that my heart is pure, my mind is stable and I make sound relationship decisions. I allow the Holy Spirit to be active in every relationship I am in. I declare that I agree with my enemies quickly. I declare that I am quick to listen and slow to speak. I declare my relationships bring me life. I declare that I benefit from being in relationship with Godly people. I declare that my relationships reflect the glory of God. I boldly confess that I am not just a receiver but I am also a giver in my relationships.

6-I boldly confess and declare that my children are a blessing and not a curse. I declare that I will raise my children in the nurture and admonition of the Lord. I declare that I will not break the spirit of my children with anger and discouragement. I declare that I will cover my children. I declare that I am a Godly parent prepared to intercede and bless my children. I declare that I will live a life that my children can model. I declare that I will not discipline my children out of spite, but I will train my children in the ways of the Lord. I declare that I will raise a Godly and productive generation. I declare that my children are taught of the Lord and they have great peace.

7-I boldly declare that I am an asset to my company. I declare that wherever I go, whatever I do, I am first and foremost an ambassador for the Kingdom of God. I boldly confess that I am not slow in business, but I am an excellent worker. I declare that I will be honest in my workings. I declare that I will be sensitive to the Holy Spirit as the Holy Spirit opens and closes doors in my career. I declare that my work ethic brings glory to God. I declare that I am full of favor with God and man. I declare that I walk in integrity and Lord blesses me abundantly.

8-I boldly confess and declare that I have made a decision to forgiveness. I forgive those who have trespassed against me, even as my Father in Heaven has forgiven me. I declare that forgiveness is my lifestyle. I will not walk in the spirit of offense. I have great peace because I love the law of God and nothing will offend me. I declare that I am a peaceably person that does not hold grudges. I declare that my spirit is free from bitterness and resentment. I declare that I am free to love those who have hurt me. I declare that the spirit of the Lord is active in my life, causing me to forgive.

9-I boldly confess and declare that who the Son sets free is free without a doubt. I loose and denounce any and all spirits that have attached themselves to me. I close every spiritual door that I have opened through sin and negligence. I declare that I am free from alcohol. I am free from drugs. I am free from nicotine. I am free from gluttonous eating. I am free from anger. I am free from masturbation. I am free from pornography. I am free from gambling. I am free from using curse words. I am free from frivolous spending. I am from hoarding. I am free from fornication. I am free unhealthy work habits. I am free from all addictions in JESUS NAME.

10-I boldly confess that the past is OVER. I declare that I look forward and not backwards. I boldly declare that my future is good. I will not fear the terror by day. I declare my future is secure in Christ. I declare that I am pressing toward the mark that I have been called to. I declare that the thoughts and the plans that God has for me are thoughts of peace and not thoughts of evil. I declare that in everything I will give thanks. I boldly confess that I will not rehearse and rehash the past mistakes that I have made, but will speak of the successful future I will have. I speak LIFE to my future generations. I speak life to my 'tomorrow'. I speak LIFE to every area of my life. I will NOT fear what tomorrow holds.

About the Author

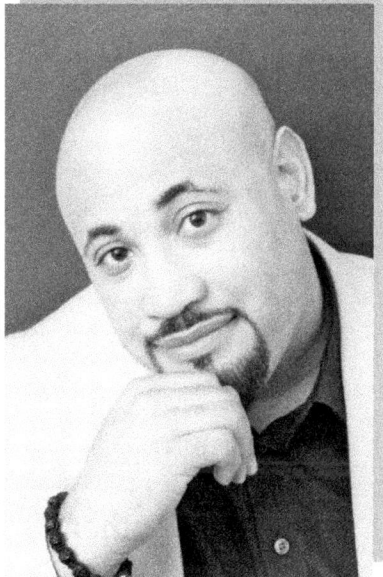

Benjamin T Moore III, serves as lead pastor and apostle of *Empowerment Church, Inc.*, (formerly Kingdom Empowerment Worship Assembly, Inc.) a city church and apostolic center established to nurture, train, equip, and release the people of God into the commission of their Kingdom Purpose.

Affectionately known as BT3, the grandson of the late Bishop Benjamin T. Moore, Sr. D.D. (Pentecostal Assemblies of the World, Inc.), this 4th generation Pastor is grounded with strong foundational roots that anchor his ability to transform lives. BT3 has ministered to hundreds with his dynamic and insightful teaching. He has an anointing to break down hindrances to total restoration and health. His exhortation is igniting; his prolific preaching is reviving; the intensity of the prophetic utterance is enlightening; and his wisdom "fathers and mentors" the body of Christ into their Kingdom Assignments.

A true heart of compassion and balance, BT3 has proven himself to be a multifaceted man of God while graciously serving in various facets of ministry leadership. Senior Chaplain with Family Chaplains Inc., he also holds membership with Trinity Evangelical. As a writer, and radio host, he is highly regarded for his community leadership and commitment to reaching the masses through the power of God. Holding a background in the Banking Industry, BT3

is no stranger to hard work and stewardship while developing small businesses that manifest power over poverty. He simply continues to make an impact that reaches across corporate, community and faith based arenas.

Founder of Advance Ministry Institute (formerly *BT3 School of Ministry*), BT3 began operating in his God given ability to identify, navigate, set vision and direction; while cultivating, equipping, training, and imparting into the followers of Jesus to advance the Kingdom of God through ministry. In 2011, BT3 was consecrated to the office of Apostle under the tutelage of his spiritual father, Apostle Byron Val Johnson, Overseer of New Wineskin Ministries Intl. It is by Divine appointment that today, the call and power of God is being demonstrated in the life of Apostle Benjamin T Moore III, as a major placeholder of regional change and transformation for the whole state of Indiana and beyond.

Apostle Benjamin T Moore III received his education at Indiana University -Purdue University at Indianapolis, Aenon Bible College (Indiana), and Wheaton College (Illinois). Currently he resides in Indianapolis with his lovely and anointed wife Lisa Michelle; and son Christopher Thomas.

BT3 Publishing
2192 E. 54th St.
Indianapolis, IN. 46220
www.bt3ministries.com

Empowerment Keys:

Wisdom to Empower &

Encourage YOU